W9-BSR-883

TO:

FROM:

Praise for **CARMINE GALLO** and *Talk Like TED*:

"*Talk Like TED* is a smart, practical book that will teach you how to give a kick-butt presentation. But Gallo goes deeper than mere instruction. This book is ultimately about discovering what moves you and then creating the means of moving others with your vision."

—Daniel H. Pink, #1 *New York Times* bestselling author of *To Sell Is Human* and *Drive*

"Inspire, motivate, and persuade any audience! That's what Carmine Gallo helped me do, and now he can help you too. Your success depends on your ability to pitch and present your vision, ideas, and proposals. Learn to deliver like a pro."

—Darren Hardy, former publisher and founding editor of *SUCCESS* magazine

10 SIMPLE SECRETS

OF THE WORLD'S GREATEST BUSINESS COMMUNICATORS

CARMINE GALLO

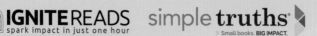

Photo Credits
Internal images © end sheets, grapegeek/Getty Images; end sheets, blackred/Getty Images; page viii, 104, Caiaimage/Martin Barraud/Getty Images; page xii, xvii, 94, 107, Hero Images/Getty Images; page xiv, Tom Werner/Getty Images; page 3, 10'000 Hours/Getty Images; page 4, Caiaimage/Agnieszka Olek/Getty Images; page 8, Westend61/Getty Images; page 14, mihailomilovanovic/Getty Images; page 38, Django/Getty Images; page 41, Caiaimage/TomMerton/Getty Images; page 53, Caiaimage/Chris Cross/Getty Images; page 70, sanjeri/Getty Images; page 73, Luis Alvarez/Getty Images; page 79, Maskot/Getty Images; page 83, Thomas Barwick/Getty Images; page 116, Aja Koska/Getty Images
Internal images on pages xviii, xxi, xxii, 19, 28, 42, 48, 60, 74, 84, and 115 have been provided by Pexels, Pixabay, or Unsplash; these images are licensed under CC0 Creative Commons and have been released by the author for public use.
Internal images on pages 65 and 108 are in the public domain.

Published by Simple Truths, an imprint of Sourcebooks
P.O. Box 4410, Naperville, Illinois 60567-4410
(630) 961-3900
sourcebooks.com

Printed and bound in China.
OGP 10 9 8 7 6 5 4 3 2 1

DEDICATED TO
VANESSA,
WHO ALWAYS BELIEVED
IN US.

TABLE OF

CONTENTS

INTRODUCTION:
Your Story. My Passion.

> **"When you change the way you see yourself as a speaker, the speaker your audience sees will change."**
> —CARMINE GALLO

You have an extraordinary story to tell. But whether you're pitching a service, product, company, or cause, how you craft and deliver your message makes all the difference. Some people tell their stories better than others—capturing the hearts and minds of everyone in their personal and professional lives. They are considered the world's greatest business communicators—the most electrifying speakers in the corporate world. **Here's the best part. Anyone can develop the skills to join the world's most astonishing speakers.** Great communicators are made, not born. In this book, you'll learn the 10 Simple Secrets that have turned ordinary individuals into dazzling presenters. You'll hear directly from the world's top contemporary business leaders, many of whom reveal their communication secrets for the first time.

By identifying and adopting the techniques of the world's greatest business communicators, you will:

▶ stand apart from your competition;

▶ attract customers;

▶ close more sales;

▶ raise your visibility;

▶ advance your business agenda;

▶ inspire your audiences; and

▶ potentially change the world with your service, product, company, or cause.

Consider just a few of the leaders who will share their secrets with you: a man who took his passion for coffee and transformed nearly every street corner in America, an investor who became the world's richest person, and a young woman who leveraged a $1,000 loan to build a billion-dollar real estate empire. They go by rather common names like Howard, Warren, and Barbara. But the companies they built are extraordinary, with names like Starbucks, Berkshire Hathaway, and the Corcoran Group.

Others have ordinary beginnings but enjoy

astounding success. There are many, many more. You'll learn about the presentation and speaking techniques of the world's most influential leaders and how you can incorporate their strategies in your own professional business communications. You'll read interviews with leading CEOs, executives, entrepreneurs, venture capitalists, experts, and authors. For the first time, they share presentation secrets that have catapulted them to the top of their fields.

Lincoln Never Used PowerPoint; He Had a Tree Stump Instead

Show me a movement that changed the world, and I'll show you a great communicator who made it happen. For example, long before Lincoln crafted and delivered the Gettysburg Address—the short speech known as one of the greatest of all time—he honed his storytelling experience on the American frontier. If it hadn't been for Lincoln's skill as a communicator, he wouldn't have won the presidency, he wouldn't have signed the

Emancipation Proclamation, and America might look far different than it does today.

In *Team of Rivals*, Pulitzer Prize–winning historian Doris Kearns Goodwin credits Lincoln's storytelling skills as a key component of his success. "Storytelling played a central role in the president's ability to communicate with the public," she writes.

Lincoln's reputation as a great communicator

attracted townspeople from far and wide to watch a magnificent storyteller captivate their imagination. Lincoln didn't have PowerPoint to lean on. Lincoln didn't have a TED stage to share his ideas with the world. All he had was tree stump and a fierce drive to improve his public-speaking skills. Great communicators inform, illuminate, and inspire on any platform.

Communication Skills Are Fundamental in the Digital Age

Communication skills are "dramatically more important" today than they were twenty years ago, according to former Cisco CEO John Chambers, whom I interviewed for a column in Forbes.com. His track record is nothing short of astonishing. In his twenty years as CEO, Chambers grew the networking company from four hundred employees to seventy thousand and from $70 million in sales to $47 billion a year.

Chambers built a reputation for electrifying audiences around the world with a captivating speaking style. Although he delivers presentations about complex topics, he makes the audience feel as though he's having a one-on-one conversation with each and every person. He walks among the audience and can speak for up to an hour with no notes.

As I learned in a candid and revealing conversation with Chambers at his Silicon Valley home, he wasn't always a confident speaker. "I am not a natural public

speaker," he acknowledged. "Between the challenges of dyslexia and a deep fear of public speaking, it did not come easy to me. It was really hard to get over."

Dyslexia made it hard for Chambers to follow written notes or read a teleprompter. But the learning disorder turned out be an asset when Chambers realized he could see the outline of the entire presentation in his mind's eye and deliver the content in a far more conversational style that made him stand out among his peers. Today, Chambers says, "communication is one of the most important skills that a leader and, frankly, most employees now need to excel on the job."

According to Chambers, one or two decades ago, a leader could get by without being an exceptional communicator and still be considered great. Today it's a different world. If you don't have communication skills, you're not going to be an effective leader.

Whether you're a CEO, manager, entrepreneur, or educator, presentations are critical to your career success. Think about how many presentations you give every day—face-to-face with a potential client, in the elevator with the boss, at a staff meeting, in a conference, or over the phone. You're presenting constantly. How do you come across? Are you dull or dazzling? The techniques described in the pages that follow will help you craft and deliver your message with power, passion, and persuasion.

While the vast majority of business professionals fail to rise to their full potential as communicators, I believe you can harness the 10 Simple Secrets in this book to stand alongside the world's greatest leaders—inspiring everyone in your personal or professional life to buy into your message.

PART

1

GET 'EM TO CARE

You may have an incredible story to tell, but your audiences won't listen if you don't build rapport with them first. They have to like you. If they feel a connection to you, they'll listen. Contemporary audiences crave speakers who have passion, who inspire, and who exude charisma. You'll know how to get those qualities by the end of part 1.

In this section you'll learn:

▶ how to develop a powerfully passionate presentation,

▶ how to inspire people to achieve goals they never thought possible, and

▶ how to prepare your presentation to capture your audience's attention.

Getting your audience to care requires that you identify and adopt three Simple Secrets shared by the world's greatest business communicators. Let's begin by revealing the first Simple Secret that will set the foundation for your extraordinary transformation.

SIMPLE SECRET #1

PASSION

> **"People with passion can change the world for the better."**
> —STEVE JOBS

There are few things I enjoy more than a caffe latte—double shot, nonfat. If you've ever stepped foot in a Starbucks, you know exactly what I'm talking about. What does this have to do with the world's greatest business communicators? Plenty. The leader who created the modern Starbucks is one of the most passionate speakers you'll ever meet.

During a now-famous trip to Italy, on a piazza in Milan, Howard Schultz's life would be forever changed upon his first sip of espresso and steamed milk.

The Italians were passionate about their coffee, he excitedly told his wife. Schultz brought that passion back to America and transformed a small Seattle coffee-bean store into an American institution. As the former chairman and CEO of Starbucks, Schultz became a billionaire and altered the habits of millions of people who visit one of Starbucks's thirty thousand locations around the world.

Schultz majored in communications, took public-speaking courses, and credits much of his ability to win over investors, customers, and employees to his sharply honed presentation skills. Before I interviewed Schultz, I read his bestselling business book *Pour Your Heart into It*. I was struck by the fact that the word "passion" appears on nearly every other page. His passion is authentic because his enthusiasm and energy carry over into his presentations—to shareholders, employees, or writers like me.

Schultz doesn't leave his passion on the pages of a book. "You either have a tremendous love for what you do, and passion for it, or you don't," Schultz told me. "Whether I'm talking to a barista, a customer, or investor, I really communicate how I feel about our company, our mission, and our values. I've said this for twenty years—it's our collective passion that provides a competitive advantage in the marketplace because we love what we do and we're inspired to do it better. We want to exceed the expectations of our people and our customers. In order to do that, you have to have a passionate commitment to everything. Everything matters, Carmine. When you're around people who share a collective passion around a common purpose, there's no telling what you can do."

The Passion Quotient

Nearly everyone can increase what I call the "Passion Quotient," or PQ—the energy and enthusiasm you exhibit as a speaker. The higher your PQ, the more likely you are to build a strong rapport with your listeners.

At its core, passion simply means this: touching the hearts of your listeners by identifying a deep emotional connection to your story and sharing that enthusiasm with your listeners. This is the Simple Secret behind building a strong rapport with your audience—whether it's an audience of one or one thousand.

Unbridled Enthusiasm

The dictionary defines *passion* as "unbridled enthusiasm." *Enthusiasm* first found its way into the English language in 1603 and literally meant "possession by a god." Its contemporary definition is "a strong liking for something." You probably wouldn't be doing what you're doing if you didn't like it. At least I hope you haven't settled for that path in life. I haven't met you but I'm making an assumption—you wouldn't be trying to improve your skills as a communicator unless you truly and deeply care about the ideas you wish to share. So I'm assuming you have a strong liking for the story you want to share, but are you possessed by it? The world's greatest business communicators are. And they show it. Share your excitement about your service, product, company, or cause. Passion is contagious.

It's Not in the Beans

The simplest way to show enthusiasm is to identify and share your emotional connection to your message. Dig deep to find your own personal connection to your story. Remember, the secret to discovering your passion is to find the object of your enthusiasm. Let's be clear on this—the object of Howard Schultz's enthusiasm isn't the sweet aroma of dark-roasted coffee beans. It's the sense of community he creates in each Starbucks store, the "third place between work and home," as he likes to call it. It's his enthusiasm about creating a company that treats employees with dignity. Community fuels his passion. It's not in the beans.

In my bestselling book *The Presentation Secrets of Steve Jobs*, I spoke to leaders who worked side-by-side with the visionary Apple cofounder. They all agree that Jobs was the greatest business communicator of our time. Jobs was an inspiring communicator precisely because he knew what business he was in. He wasn't in the business of selling computers; he was passionate about building tools that would unleash people's creativity. Jobs was a master salesman because he didn't sell products—he sold dreams. And dreams are always more intoxicating than products.

The first step to becoming a great communicator is the simplest—you cannot inspire unless you're inspired yourself. Dig deep to find your passion, and don't be afraid to express it.

1 Study great speakers. Watch an eighteen-minute TED Talk or a keynote presentation by a successful CEO or business leader. Ask yourself:

   ▸ How can I tell they're passionate about the topic?

   ▸ What is their connection to the topic?

   ▸ Do they convey energy, enthusiasm, and excitement on stage?

2 Connect to your topic. Becoming a passionate speaker will be easier if you understand your personal and emotional connection to your topic. By answering the following questions, you'll be using your head to reach the hearts of your listeners:

   ▸ Why do you believe in your service, product, company, or cause? Why should your listeners care?

▶ What's your connection to your story? Think about your background, childhood or adulthood experiences, encounters with colleagues, anecdotes, etc.

▶ Have you shared this connection with your audience? If not, how can you incorporate it into your message?

INSPIRATION

"I can inspire people to
do things I believe in."

—MICHAEL JORDAN

Few visions have had as profound an impact as Nelson
Mandela's "dream of an Africa which is in peace with
itself." Mandela spent more than twenty-seven years in
prison for fighting to improve the plight of black South
Africa during a time of white minority rule. Mandela
was set free after South Africa abolished apartheid. He

was awarded the Nobel Peace Prize and served as the first black South African president after winning the country's first multiracial election.

The years he spent in a notorious Cape Town prison only strengthened his resolve to change the way his countrymen lived together. His vision saw him through those years and inspired hundreds of millions of people in South Africa and around the world. Your vision might not be as grand as a world in which race and color don't matter, but it proves that a big and bold vision cannot be underestimated.

Mandela had a road map: he knew where he wanted to lead his people and how to get there. What's your road map? Where do you want to take your company? How will you get there? Above all, have you communicated this vision to the people who serve with you? Mandela painted a compelling vision. He was an artist who transformed the hopes and aspirations of the people who followed him. By painting a compelling vision of a bright future, you too can lead others in your mission.

The world's greatest communicators paint pictures by telling inspiring stories. You'll find that each of the extraordinary business communicators interviewed for this book uses stories to paint a vivid picture of their vision.

The very first line of Howard Schultz's book has nothing to do with Starbucks but in a sense has everything to do with it. The first sentence of *Pour Your Heart into It* reads, "On a cold January day in 1961, my father broke his ankle at work." The story of how his father's injury left his family with no income, no insurance, and no safety net to cushion the blow marked a turning point in Schultz's life.

Schultz consistently tells this story to employees, journalists, and shareholders as a way of inspiring his audiences to back his vision. I wanted to know more about that story when I spoke to Schultz.

"What does your dad's experience have to do with roasting coffee beans?" I asked.

"On many levels, the experiences I had as a young

child formed my values and my understanding of what it meant for people to be left behind," Schultz responded.

"Starbucks employs eighty thousand people. We hire three hundred people a day and open three new stores a day. It's very important new people understand that when I started this company I had nothing—what drove me then and what drives me today is to build a different type of company, to create an environment in which people are respected and dignified in the workplace. Starbucks is the quintessential people-based business. I've always thought it was important that people have a sense of my own vulnerability as well as what it is we're trying to achieve as a business.

"It goes against the past tradition of business leaders who kept personal stories private, but it's important that people understand who you are, why you act a certain way and respond to things in a certain way. If you look at some of the great leaders in history, they had the gift of galvanizing large groups because

people saw in them something that resonated. To do that, you have to let people in—take off the shield."

In today's world, authenticity matters a lot. Employees look for authentic leaders to work for, and customers look for authentic brands to buy from. It's more important than ever for contemporary communicators to let people in, to "take off the shield."

One of the top CEO recruiters in the world, Spencer Stuart's James Citrin, agrees that Schultz inspires by sharing stories.

"The story about his father—it provides the underpinning for stock options and full health benefits for all employees, even part-timers," says Citrin.

"When he tells the story about how he went on vacation to Italy, got entranced by the espresso-bar culture, and believed that he could transport that kind of community—that was the seed of the Starbucks strategy. He brings the stories to life. To get the most out of people they're working with, leaders have to tap into their emotions as well as their minds. People can relate to stories. They can see themselves in other people's stories. I would bet that when Howard Schultz introduced the Bean Stock program [stock options to turn employees into partners] in a board meeting, he told the story about his father. The ability to use stories to get people to buy in with their hearts is a powerful leadership capability."

In 2001, a group of researchers from four American universities conducted an exhaustive analysis of presidential speeches to determine why some were more charismatic than others. What they found was extraordinary, but of no surprise to anyone who understands why the great business communicators profiled in this book radiate magnetism. The study, published in *Administrative Science Quarterly*, concludes, "The successful articulation and enactment of a leader's vision may rest on his or her ability to paint followers a verbal picture of what can be accomplished with their help."

According to the study, the most effective way of

painting a verbal picture involves the use of image-based rhetoric. "Leaders who use words that evoke pictures, sounds, smells, tastes, and other sensations tap more directly into followers' life experiences than do leaders who use words that appeal solely to followers' intellects." In other words, charismatic leaders use words that evoke sensory experiences to connect on an emotional level—words like "dream," "sweat," and "heart."

Great contemporary business communicators are masters of using vivid imagery.

Image-based words will help you win over your audience for several reasons:

▶ You'll grab and keep their attention. Images are concrete. Abstract concepts are harder to follow and tougher to remember. They fail to inspire.

▶ You'll stick with your audience long after your talk. People can't act on something they don't remember. Vivid images inspire. They are richer experiences that will stick in the minds of your listeners.

▶ You'll reach their hearts. Most people will not act on messages that fail to connect with them on an emotional level. According to the research, "Leaders who infuse their messages with image-based words will, therefore, evoke a stronger emotional response among followers, increasing followers' willingness to embrace their visions and, ultimately, to act."

The Big Mission: First Why, Not How

People crave direction, and they're more than willing to take the road less traveled as long as they know why they're taking the road.

Great business communicators share the why before the how. Apple founder and CEO Steve Jobs was a master of inspiration. He radiated a stage presence that captivated thousands of the "Mac faithful" as well as customers, employees, and colleagues. Jobs cofounded Apple in 1976 and ignited the personal computer revolution by launching the Apple II and the Macintosh. After a long exile from the company he formed, Jobs made a dramatic return to Apple in 1997 and nurtured it back to health. Jobs was Apple's CEO as well as CEO of Pixar, the award-winning animation studio, now a subsidiary of Disney.

Jobs had a reputation as being one of the most captivating pitchmen in corporate history. According to Alan Deutschman in *The Second Coming of Steve Jobs*, "He was the master at taking something that might be considered boring—a hunk of electronic hardware—and enveloping it in a story that made it compellingly dramatic." Whether at Apple or Pixar, people wanted to work for Jobs because they found his big mission intoxicating.

Sell Sugared Water or Change the World

Jobs incorporated many subtle techniques into his presentations (techniques that will be revealed in coming chapters), but the key to his success as a communicator was his nearly messianic zeal to change the world. Jobs passionately believed that he was not creating merely a computer but a tool to help people unleash their creativity. By painting a compelling vision of the future, Jobs persuaded bright people to work for him, investors to believe in him, and customers to buy from him.

I interviewed former Apple CEO John Sculley and asked whether a popular legend was true. He assured me it did happen. In March 1983, the brash twenty-eight-year-old Jobs was sitting on a terrace overlooking the Hudson River with forty-four-year-old John Sculley, then president of Pepsi. In an effort to recruit Sculley to Apple, Jobs turned to him and said, "Do you want to spend the rest of your life selling sugared water, or do you want a chance to change the world?" That's bold. That's optimistic. That's a big mission.

Sculley said the question landed like a punch to the gut. He accepted.

Describing a big mission simply, concisely, and passionately is important to telling inspiring stories. Jobs didn't have trouble raising capital in his life because he knew how to share his big mission.

All great business communicators have a big mission they use to inspire, motivate, and persuade their audiences.

Does your vision inspire you? If not, it's time to reevaluate the big mission behind your service, product, company, or cause. After all, if you're not out to change the world, there are plenty who are. Before you build your next presentation or create a pitch to sell your idea, ask yourself the following questions:

1. Who do you consider inspiring? How does that person "paint a picture"? How does that person paint a picture of a better world?

2 What relevant stories can you share? What stories can you incorporate in your next presentation? Make them personal and vivid. How do they connect to the mission of your service, product, company, or cause?

3 What's your big mission? Remember, your big mission is not to sell me ten thousand units of your widget. It's to sell me on a dream—how will your product, service, or company make me money? How will it make me more productive or help me retain employees? Show me how your idea will solve my problems, and you'll win me over.

SIMPLE SECRET #3

PREPARATION

> ## "The more I practice the luckier I get."
> —GARY PLAYER

If you want to achieve unbelievable things in your personal or professional life, you need to have a bold vision (your big mission) and an unshakable belief in your ability to reach your goal. Even with a grand vision, great business communicators take it one step further. They get their audiences to buy into their vision by first learning what the audiences want, need, and expect. They do their homework first. Not one of the speakers I interviewed for this book starts a presentation without knowing more about their audience than most people know about their neighbors. They ask themselves a series of questions that allows them to build a strong rapport with their listeners before they've said their first words.

The Three Questions You Must Ask Yourself

The world's greatest business communicators get to know their audience before they say a single word. So should you. Let me make it even easier for you by listing three questions you should ask yourself before any type of public presentation—whether it's a meeting with your boss, a client pitch, a product launch, or a media interview. Remember, you're always presenting. Answering these three simple questions about your audience will help you soar to the next level as a corporate speaker:

1 What do they need to know?

2 Why should they care?

3 What action do I want them to take?

The answers to these questions will help you master the material. In fact, if you take only one thing away from this chapter, make it these four words: "Why should I care?" Those four words are on the minds of every person in your audience—a boss, a board, a sales prospect, it doesn't matter. Have you ever been bored to tears while watching a presentation at a conference but considered it rude to leave since you were sitting in the front row? Painful, isn't it? If the presenter had simply asked one question— "Why should my audience care?"—you may have survived the presentation or, better yet, actually enjoyed it! If the presenter had asked himself the other two questions, you might have enjoyed it and given the speaker your business. Now that's a winning presentation.

It's that simple. By asking three questions about your audience, you can easily establish a rapport with your listeners—getting 'em to care about your message. Remember, your goal is to get your audience to nod in agreement and to genuinely want to hear more. It's to be heard!

Rehearse, Rehearse, Rehearse

Once you know your audience, rehearsing is the second and final action to mastering your material. Glancing at notes two minutes before your presentation won't cut it. Rehearsing means walking through your talk or presentation exactly as you would when you deliver it.

Harvard brain researcher Dr. Jill Bolte Taylor gave a TED Talk that went viral. Millions of viewers were amazed by her "My Stroke of Insight" presentation where she described how she analyzed her own stroke—as she was experiencing it. What they didn't see was the enormous amount of preparation Bolte Taylor put into it. She rehearsed the eighteen-minute presentation about two hundred times before she delivered it on stage. Practice relentlessly and internalize the content so you can deliver it as comfortably as having a conversation with a friend.

Put In the Effort to Look Effortless

Great communicators practice relentlessly. They've internalized the content, so they keep their eyes focused on the audience and not the slides.

Reciting facts, figures, and statistics is nearly impossible for most of us to do without looking down at notes or slides. It's perfectly acceptable to glance away from the audience every now and then. But your introduction, your conclusion, and 90 percent of everything in between should be delivered by looking directly into the eyes of your audience. The only way to accomplish this feat—the *only* way—is to practice until you know the main message of each slide by heart.

Above all, don't read. That's why television anchors use teleprompters, so they can look directly at their viewers. Unfortunately, most presenters will spend the majority of their time reading from slides or notes instead of using those notes solely as guideposts.

Video Is Your Best Preparation Tool

Rehearsing should be an important part of your preparation routine, and that includes seeing yourself on video. Any smartphone will do the trick.

Watching yourself is an easy way to get rid of visual or audible distractions like poor eye contact, irritating gestures, bad posture, or annoying habits (like using too many "ums" and "ahs" when you talk).

And practice, practice, practice. In front of a mirror, in front of a colleague. I think it's a mistake to make an important presentation without at least ten run-throughs of the entire presentation. As a side benefit, you'll grow more confident with each rehearsal.

Watch yourself on video. Record your presentation and watch it back. If possible, find objective friends or colleagues who will give you honest feedback. Here's what I would look for:

▸ Ask yourself, "Does this person engage me? Do I want to hear more? Is she/he convincing? Genuine? Passionate?" (Simple Secret #1)

▸ How's your energy level? You might feel as though you're enthusiastic about the topic, but the video doesn't lie—it will show whether you look like you've just rolled out of bed on a Sunday morning or you're truly engaged, enthusiastic, and electrifying! (Simple Secrets #1 and #9)

▶ Do you get to the point quickly, or do you tend to meander from thought to thought? Is your message clear or convoluted? (Simple Secrets #5 and #6)

▶ What does your body language say? Do you exude strong, confident, and commanding body language? Are your arms crossed instead of open? Do you fidget, rock, or have other distracting body mannerisms? If so, the video will help you identify bad habits and eliminate them. (Simple Secret #8)

▶ Do you use comfortable, animated, and purposeful hand gestures, or do you look stiff and wooden? (Simple Secret #8)

▶ Do you have nonsense or filler words that you repeat all the time while you're thinking? (Simple Secret #7)

▷ How do you look? Is your wardrobe disheveled or crisp? Do the colors you wear complement your skin tone, or do you look washed out? Do you look a little better than the people in your audience? (Simple Secret #9)

Your audience won't follow you until they like you, unless and until they feel as though they have a deeper relationship with you. The more meaningful the relationship, the more receptive they'll be to your message. Once you've gotten your audience to care about your message by being passionate, inspirational, and prepared, it's time to grab 'em and keep 'em by identifying the next three Simple Secrets of great communicators.

PART

2

GRAB 'EM AND
KEEP 'EM

Once you've built rapport with your audience, they'll
be receptive to your message. But now what? You've
got to grab 'em, keep 'em interested, and, most importantly, get them to take a desired action—whether it's
to use your service, buy your product, invest in your
company, or support your cause.

The great business communicators who reveal their
secrets in this section will teach you how to:

▶ captivate your audience in the first few seconds;

▶ articulate a simple, clear, and compelling message anyone can understand; and

▶ earn a reputation for being a spokesperson who is not only clear but also concise.

Grabbing and keeping your audience's attention requires that you start strong, end strong, make it clear, and keep it brief. So here we go—Simple Secret #4!

SIMPLE SECRET #4

START STRONG

> **"A powerful beginning and ending will stick with your listeners."**
> —OPRAH WINFREY

If you were to show someone a group of photos of fruits like an apple, pear, peach, plum, and pomegranate, what are they most likely to remember? Studies have shown that people recall the first and last items on the list—the apple and the pomegranate. It works the same in presentations. People tend to remember the first thing you say and the last.

Barbara Corcoran, one of the stars of the hit show *Shark Tank*, says that in 80 percent of the pitches she hears on the show she knows whether she's in or out in the first minute. Corcoran's not alone. Most audiences make up their mind about a speaker before the first sixty seconds are over.

Don't Bury the Lead

In journalism, when the headline of a story is buried somewhere in the middle of it, we call it "burying the lead." It's a no-no. The same is true when pitching, promoting, or presenting—if you're speaking for fifteen minutes on a particular subject and you wait fourteen minutes before announcing the headline, or key message, of your topic, you've already lost your listeners. In fact, they probably started looking at their watches long ago.

When journalists introduce a story, it's called the

lead. In television, it's typically no longer than 15–30 seconds. It's meant to be so intriguing that you'll want to hear the rest of the story. If all the leads are interesting, you'll stick with the entire newscast.

The easiest way to develop a strong opening for your next presentation, talk, pitch, or meeting is simply to create a compelling lead that you can say in thirty seconds. If you can say it in twenty seconds, even better. The lead should be a short description of your service, product, company, or cause that your grandmother could understand. It must be clear, concise, and compelling. The world's greatest business communicators have their leads down cold. You can too.

Now let's get started crafting a thirty-second lead you can call your own—whether you're pitching a service, product, company, cause, or yourself! After spending the past twenty years immersed in the study of public speaking and communication, I've arrived at four questions that need to be answered quickly in a presentation, pitch, or job interview. They are:

1 What is my service, product, company, or cause?

2 What problem do I solve?

3 How am I different?

4 Why should you care?

The human brain evolved to see the big picture before getting immersed in the details. By answering these four questions, your audience will get the gist of your idea. Once you've grabbed your listeners' attention and they want to hear more, it's time to make sure your message is heard by revealing the fifth Simple Secret of the world's greatest business communicators. Keep in mind:

1 Craft your thirty-second lead. Don't open PowerPoint or build a slide until you've answered the following questions in one or two sentences:

What is my product, what problem does it solve, how is it different, and why should my audience care?

2. Time yourself. Use a stopwatch to keep your pitch concise. You should be able to deliver your lead in thirty seconds or less. Sixty seconds won't hurt, but it's a good discipline to keep it shorter.

SIMPLE SECRET #5

CLARITY

> **"Insecure managers create complexity... Real leaders don't need clutter."**
>
> —JACK WELCH

The movie *Black Hawk Down* captures the heroic struggle of 160 U.S. soldiers caught in a harrowing battle with 10,000 enemy fighters during a mission in Mogadishu, Somalia, on October 3, 1993. It's an inspiring movie, portraying the discipline, courage, and loyalty of elite soldiers who live by a simple code—no one gets left behind.

I've had several conversations with the commander in charge of that mission, Sgt. Matt Eversmann. Effective communication is at the heart of his leadership course at Johns Hopkins University.

Military missions are extraordinarily complicated, requiring immense coordination, preparation, and rehearsal. But when communicating orders to ground forces, great military leaders keep it short, simple, and clear. For example, the operation in Somalia required seventeen helicopters that could fly over only certain areas of the city and twenty vehicles that could drive only in specific parts, and they all needed to be in precise coordination. According to Eversmann, in every mission each soldier knows his role but doesn't have to know all the moving pieces. It's the commander's job to cut the clutter. Eversmann's orders to his soldiers just before the Somalia mission could not have been simpler: "Surround the building, keep the bad guys out of our target area while our assault force does its stuff, and move out by air." Great leaders reinforce their messages...clearly.

Leaders on the front lines of any industry must strive for simplicity and clarity if they hope to inspire and motivate employees, customers, or shareholders.

Twenty-First-Century Communicators

If you're thinking to yourself, "That's great, Carmine, but our product is far too complicated to talk about in simple terms," you're wrong. That attitude will destroy your ability to connect with contemporary audiences. Albert Einstein once said that "any fool" can make things more complex. The true genius makes it simpler. He was right. If you're truly committed to transforming your audiences with your presentations, then you have no choice but to craft your message so everyone can grasp its implications.

Clarity Can Make Your Stock Soar

Great business communicators use three techniques to make their messages clear:

1. They ask themselves, "Where's the Wow?"

2. They cut the jargon.

3. They dress up their message with story enhancers.

Where's the Wow?

Jack Welch is the one of the most admired and influential CEOs in the world. During his twenty years as GE's top executive, the conglomerate grew from $13 billion in revenue to $500 billion. Welch was on a mission to "declutter" everything about the company, from its management processes to its communication. He hated long and convoluted memos, meetings, and presentations.

In his book *Jack: Straight from the Gut*, Welch discusses the initial meetings he had with division leaders that left him "underwhelmed." Clutter and jargon had no place in his meetings. If you wanted to upset the new CEO, just talk over his head. Welch would ask, "Let's pretend we're in high school… Take me through the basics." Welch recalls his first meeting with one of his insurance leaders. Welch asked some simple questions about terms he was unfamiliar with. Welch writes, "So I interrupted him to ask: 'What's the difference between facultative and treaty insurance?' After fumbling through a long answer for several minutes, an answer I wasn't getting, he finally blurted out in exasperation, 'How do you expect me to teach you in five minutes what it has taken me twenty-five years to learn!' Needless to say, he didn't last long."

Finding the Wow

Journalists are trained to filter through the most complicated subjects to find the Wow: the essence of the story that makes readers, viewers, or listeners perk up and pay attention. In journalism school, instructors asked me, "Where's the Wow?" I used it throughout my career. If a press release or pitch didn't pass the Wow Test, we'd throw it out. The Wow is the one thing that will make your audience sit up and pay attention. Whether your audience is made up of journalists, customers, or colleagues, everyone is looking for the Wow.

In 2001, Steve Jobs pulled a small MP3 player out of his pocket. The first iPod stored "a thousand songs in your pocket," the first portable music player that could do it. That's a Wow moment. In 2008, to prove that the new MacBook Air was the "world's thinnest notebook," Jobs walked to the side of the stage and took out a manila envelope for all to see. He reached inside and pulled out the new computer. That's a Wow moment.

A Wow moment doesn't have to be a prop. It can be story, a demo, or an interesting graphic. Above all, in one slide or with one prop, it tells an entire story.

Lose the Jargon or Lose Your Audience

Great business communicators avoid mind-numbing jargon, especially when delivering to outsiders the message behind their service, product, company, or cause. It's not an option anymore to take your language down to a very simple, clear, and understandable level. Remove any words that most people will not understand. Jargon gets in the way of clarity.

During a conversation with former Apple Macintosh evangelist Guy Kawasaki, the venture capital investor told me that entrepreneurs often lose a pitch the minute they start adding adjectives that sound like every other entrepreneur pitching investors that day. "I wish I had a dollar for every time I heard a pitch for a 'revolutionary, patent-pending, curve-jumping, innovative, scalable, enterprise-class product created by rock-star programmers,'" he said. Needless to say, adjective-laden pitches aren't memorable precisely because they all sound the same. Why, then, do entrepreneurs and business professionals insist on using convoluted, meaningless buzzwords? The answer—fear.

The Fear That Leads to Jargon

Suze Orman built a financial advice empire with books and television shows. She did so by taking complex financial advice and turning it into language that most people could understand.

"Too many people want to impress others with the information they have so others think the speaker is intelligent," she once told me.

"Here's the key. You must not be afraid of criticism. If your intention is to impart a message that will create change for the person listening, then if you ask me, it is respectful to that person to make the message as simple as possible. For example, if I gave you directions to how to get to my house, you would want me to give you the simplest directions to get there. If I made it more complicated, you would not be better off. You might get aggravated and give up. If it were simple, chances are you will get in your car and try to get to my house rather than giving up and saying it's not worth it. Others criticize simplicity because they need to feel that it's more complicated. If everything were so simple, they think their jobs could be eliminated. It's our fear of extinction, our fear of elimination, our fear of not being important that leads us to communicate things in a more complex way than we need to."

Imagine what you could accomplish if you sold your ideas more persuasively: raise your visibility, inspire your employees, attract investors, and make more sales. The world's greatest business communicators have this ability because they've mastered the fifth Simple Secret. They keep their messages simple and clear. A simple message is easier to remember. And a message that's easier to remember is easier to act on.

Now that it's clear that clarity is key, it's time to reveal the sixth Simple Secret of all great business communicators.

But first, eliminate the following buzzwords from your presentation…and don't replace them with others!

▶ at the end of the day   ▶ next-generation

▶ benchmark   ▶ paradigm-shifting

▶ best of breed   ▶ robust

▶ best practices   ▶ scalable

▶ core competencies   ▶ solution(s)

▶ deliverables   ▶ synergy

▶ end user   ▶ value-added

▶ leading-edge   ▶ win-win

▶ mission-critical

SIMPLE SECRET #6

BREVITY

John F. Kennedy galvanized the nation in 1961 with an inaugural address scripted for fifteen minutes. Think about it. In fifteen minutes, Kennedy shared a vision that inspired generations, changed social policies in the sixties, and inspired a nation to land a man on the moon by the end of the decade. The world's greatest communicators, in business or politics, keep it brief.

The most persuasive speakers are their own best editors. They cut, cut, and cut some more. In his magnificent book about the Kennedy years, *A Thousand Days*, Arthur Schlesinger said Kennedy "was an excellent editor, skilled at tuning up thoughts and eliminating verbal excess." In *Kennedy*, JFK's primary speechwriter, Ted Sorensen, wrote that Kennedy would use one-syllable words instead of three-syllable words when appropriate, or one word instead of two or three words to say the same thing. The inauguration speech is on display at the Kennedy library near Boston. You can see where Kennedy crossed out the word "adversaries" and replaced it with "foe." Kennedy kept his speeches—his presentations—as tight as possible. Actually, it was George Washington who set the tone for brevity. His second inaugural address was only 135 words!

Now ask yourself, "Do I really need sixty minutes

and fifty-two PowerPoint slides to tell the story behind my service, product, company, or cause? Can I cut something out?" I'll bet you can, and your presentation will be stronger for it.

The Window of Impact

The public's desire for brevity is universal. Nobody wants to hear you ramble. The famous TED Talk conference has a hard-and-fast rule for all presenters, no matter how famous the name. No speaker can present for longer than eighteen minutes. After more than thirty years of experience, the TED organizers conclude that eighteen minutes is long enough to have a serious discussion about a topic and short enough to hold the audience's attention.

When it comes to presentations, ten to eighteen minutes is what I call the "Window of Impact" to get your message across. Studies have shown that our attention span isn't that long. Audience attention drops off dramatically after approximately ten minutes to eighteen minutes. After that point, your listeners' brains experience "cognitive backlog." It's like holding out your arms while someone else piles on weights. At some point, you'll drop everything.

The long-running television news program *60 Minutes* runs, well, an hour. But each segment is about fifteen minutes. Kennedy's inaugural speech ran fifteen minutes. Steve Jobs's famous Stanford commencement speech lasted fifteen minutes. And Martin Luther King Jr.'s famous "I Have a Dream" speech came in at seventeen minutes.

If Kennedy and King can inspire a nation in under twenty minutes, you can certainly cover your topic in that time.

The Short Story of NYC's Broker to the Stars

Barbara Corcoran is a motivational dynamo, a great speaker, very wealthy, and a famous television personality on ABC's *Shark Tank*, the show where entrepreneurs pitch their ideas to a panel of investors.

She started New York's premier real estate firm, the Corcoran Group, with a $1,000 loan from a boyfriend. The relationship fizzled but the loan grew. Twenty-five years later, the Corcoran Group grew to $5 billion in sales thanks, in large part, to Corcoran's ability to touch the hearts and minds of her clients. Corcoran has since sold the Corcoran Group to NRT for a reported $70 million. Not a bad return for a $1,000 loan.

Corcoran spent a lot of time with me as we tried to identify the secrets behind her success as a communicator. Like most of the personalities interviewed for this book, I can talk about her in any chapter, but she has some very insightful things to say on the topic of brevity. For instance, in any communication, whether it's on the phone or behind a podium, Corcoran believes in cutting to the chase.

"People are not as interested in you as you think they are," Corcoran said.

"Once the spotlight is on you, you begin to think that you are the most important person in the room and everything you have to say is *soooo* very important. And it's just not true. I think you have to be hyper-paranoid about how succinct you are and respect the listener's time... Important people think they're very busy. But the fact of the matter is everyone is very busy. They simply don't have the time to hear the details—unless it's a story, but even then you need to get rid of the excess."

Corcoran's conversations last no longer than they have to. She especially likes to keep her speeches short. If she's scheduled to speak for thirty or forty minutes, Corcoran will speak for all of twelve minutes and spend the rest of the time answering questions. Corcoran sticks to the Window of Impact.

Twenty-Five Words or Fewer

Tech Coast Angels in Orange County, California, is one of the largest angel investor groups in the country, made up of wealthy individuals who fund promising start-up firms. The group hosts a fast-pitch contest meant to separate the potential winners from the deadly duds.

In one competition that I attended, thirty-six firms were invited to participate; twelve would get to present in front of the entire group of five hundred investors. Here's the catch: they had only sixty seconds to make their case. I couldn't help but wonder how many small firms lost the opportunity to become big firms because their spokespeople failed to make a compelling case in sixty seconds.

Here's an exercise—if you had only twenty-five words to describe your service, product, company, or cause, how would you do it? If you can't articulate the big picture behind your idea, product, or company in twenty-five words or fewer, keep editing until you can. Remember, Thomas Jefferson chose only twenty-two words as the inscription on his tombstone. It reads: "Author of the Declaration of American Independence, of the Statute of Virginia for Religious Freedom, and Father of the University of Virginia."

Jefferson left a lot out, including the fact that he served as America's second president.

I hope this chapter has helped you appreciate the power of conciseness. Respect your listeners' time by eliminating excessive words in presentations, meetings, presentations, or pitches. In turn, they will respect you and your message. You'll stand a better chance of being heard.

Now that you've learned the secrets to grabbing and keeping the attention of your listeners, it's time to reveal the last three Simple Secrets that will help you seal the deal.

3

BLOW 'EM AWAY BY TALKING, WALKING, AND LOOKING LIKE A LEADER

Now that you've successfully crafted and articulated a message your audience cares about, it's time to talk, walk, and look like a leader. The great business communicators you'll hear from in the sections on Simple Secrets #7 through #9 use their voices and bodies to capture the hearts, minds, and souls of their listeners.

The captivating tools showcased in this section will teach you how to:

▶ deliver your message with power and confidence,

▶ exude a commanding presence over everyone in the room, and

▶ dress and look like a leader people want to follow.

Let's continue your transformation by improving the way you deliver the story you've crafted. It's time to reveal Simple Secret #7.

SIMPLE SECRET **#7**

SAY IT WITH STYLE

> **"My whole career has been writing for the ear, and this is how you do it: in relatively short sentences that impart information quickly."**
> **—PEGGY NOONAN**

One Saturday night, October 11, 2003, I spent three hours at a small Italian restaurant listening to the stories of a man whose feat will never be outdone: former astronaut Neil Armstrong.

I joined Armstrong thanks to a family friend who set up dinner for a group of us. During dinner, after a few glasses of a fine Barolo, somebody in the group had the courage to ask Armstrong what all of us had been thinking: "Did you come up with 'One small step for [a] man, one giant leap for mankind,' or did someone at NASA tell you to say it?" For the record, Armstrong came up with it. During dinner, I kept thinking about those ten memorable words and how they were delivered, with just the right pause for dramatic effect: "One small step for [a] man…one giant leap for mankind." Armstrong knew instinctively what all great business communicators know—a pause at just the right time adds significance to words that the words themselves cannot express.

Great business communicators deliver their message with style. They know the impression they make often has less to do with the actual words they use than the way they deliver those words. Their tone, inflection, and speed all serve to captivate their listeners.

Poet Maya Angelou was hailed as one of the great "voices" of contemporary literature.

Angelou's words are beautiful, but Angelou's powerful delivery brought the words to life. Although she had a string of bestselling books, like *I Know Why the Caged Bird Sings*, Angelou's popularity soared when she read one of her poems, "On the Pulse of Morning," for President Bill Clinton's inauguration in 1993. Angelou brought a completely new dimension to her work by the way she used her voice. Newspaper articles written the day after the inauguration praised Angelou for her "hypnotic presence" and "powerful delivery" that left as deep an impression as her words.

You're not going to enter your next staff meeting delivering your presentation in the same deliberative, thoughtful, and dramatic fashion as Angelou read her poetry. But there is something we can all learn from Angelou. She paused at key moments, punched key words, and varied her tone and inflection. Angelou taught us that both the words we use and the way we say those words are critical to captivating our listeners.

Tone

A monotone speaker doesn't have any inflection in their voice. A monotone speaker strings words and phrases together in the same tone of voice—a dull, repetitive style of sound. It's great for Tibetan chants when you're trying to fall sleep, but it's not the best strategy for keeping your audience awake. Your voice should be like a landscape portrait with peaks and valleys, variations in pitch, volume, and inflections. Your voice should rise and fall, curve, twist, and turn. It'll mesmerize your listeners and leave them with a sense of awe.

Pace

The average American speaks at a rate of 125 to 150 words per minute. If you speak at a much faster pace, your audience will have a hard time keeping up. Speak

much slower and you'll put them to sleep. The secret is to vary the pace of your delivery.

TED speaker and human rights attorney Bryan Stevenson delivered a presentation that earned the longest standing ovation in TED history. As a persuader who has argued and won cases before the U.S. Supreme Court, he's a masterful public speaker. Stevenson constantly varies his pace to keep the audience riveted. For example, in one anecdote about meeting civil rights hero Rosa Parks, Stevenson sped up his delivery when he described what he told Parks about his nonprofit organization: "I began giving her my rap. I said, 'Well, we're trying to challenge injustice. We're trying to help people who have been wrongly convicted. We're trying to confront bias and discrimination in the administration of criminal justice. We're trying to end life without parole sentences for children. We're trying to do something about the death penalty. We're trying to reduce the prison population. We're trying to end mass incarceration.'"

Stevenson then slowed down, paused, and delivered the punchline. Parks responded: "Mmm, mmm, mmm. That's going to make you tired, tired, tired." Stevenson knows a few things about persuasion—and doesn't leave his delivery to chance.

Cross Your T's

There's a hilarious episode of *Seinfeld* called "The Puffy Shirt" in which the character Kramer brings his girlfriend to meet Jerry, Elaine, and George. They call her a "low talker" because everyone strains to hear every word the girlfriend says. Of course, they misinterpret every word. I think there's a vocal quality that's just as bad—the Mumbler!

Great business communicators clearly enunciate every word. Mumbling is one of the easiest mistakes to correct. You just need to be aware of it as you listen to yourself on video or audio. The problem most speakers have is that they fail to pronounce final consonants in words that end in "nt." Most people simply trail off, so words like "can't" sound like "can" and words like "won't" sound like "won." These are fairly simple problems to overcome. At the beginning of my career, I certainly would not have received an A for articulation. Reciting simple tongue twisters improved my enunciation. Peter Piper picked a peck of pickled peppers... it works!

By now I hope you're convinced that how you deliver your message is equally as important as the words themselves. Keep your listeners engaged by using all of the techniques of great business and broadcast speakers—varying your tone, inflections, and speed; using pauses to set aside key thoughts and phrases; and enunciating clearly.

Your magnificent delivery has pulled your audience in deeper. Let's take it up another level. It's time to reveal the eighth Simple Secret of all great business communicators.

SIMPLE SECRET #8

COMMAND PRESENCE

> "[George] Washington's bearing and presence bedazzled people... He never lounged or slouched... Washington was, quite simply, a sight to behold."
> —RON CHERNOW

Some presentations are more important than others. There are some in which failure could cost your job, your reputation, and your company. One of my clients, a top executive for a technology firm, was preparing to give a major presentation to the company's primary investor—a famous CEO who is one of the wealthiest people in the world. In addition to positive news about the product, its patents, and engineering milestones, my client also had to address an uncomfortable fact—the firm had hit a snag in the development and would have to delay the launch of a product.

That presented a slight problem—his body language. Everything about it said, "We're in deep trouble. We don't have a clue as to how to solve this glitch, and the delay might very well become permanent. I'm lost. I can't lead this team, and we'll burn through the rest of your money in no time." Of course, that wasn't the case at all. Far from it. In fact, my client's engineering team had jumped far greater hurdles in the past. They were all very confident the current stall would easily be overcome and the product would go on to become a smashing success (which it did).

I watched the executive rehearse his PowerPoint

presentation. The content on the slides wasn't the problem; the problem was with the speaker. His body language was a mess—eyes cast downward, hands awkwardly tucked in his pockets, his body swaying back and forth. This guy was a poster boy for poor body language. He seemed insecure and out of his league.

Fortunately, this story has a good ending. In addition to working on each of the 10 Simple Secrets in this book, my client eliminated bad habits and rocked the house during his presentation. He made solid eye contact with everybody in the room, he pulled his hands out of his pockets and used purposeful, assertive hand gestures. He didn't read from notes or turn his back to the audience to read from the slides. His posture and stance exuded power, confidence, and competence—he had charisma. The wealthy investor said he was pleased with the presentation and expressed confidence the project was in good hands. The executive went on to successfully navigate the issues and, later, went on to lead another company in the investor's portfolio.

Military Leaders Call Confident Body Language "Command Presence"

Leaders with "command presence" present themselves with authority and confidence, as a person who deserves respect and loyalty. Command presence comes across in how you talk, how you walk, and how you look. Are people ready to follow you as soon as you step on the stage? Does your body language convey confidence and competence? If so, you have command presence. Inspiring leaders don't slouch. They maintain eye contact. They use appropriate hand gestures. They look, talk, and walk like a person you'd want to follow when things get rough.

Entire books have been written on body language. But since this book promises you "simple secrets," here are three simple habits you can adopt today to build command presence:

1 Open posture

2 Eye contact

3 Hand gestures

Open Posture

Open posture simply means that you don't put anything between you and the listener. That includes a lectern. Don't stand behind an object if you don't have to. Here are some other changes you can make to have an open posture.

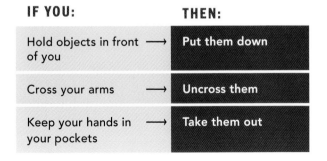

IF YOU:	THEN:
Hold objects in front of you →	Put them down
Cross your arms →	Uncross them
Keep your hands in your pockets →	Take them out

These very common habits are easy to fix. Anytime you place anything between you and the listener, you create a barrier, an unconscious defensive mechanism that indicates you're hiding something—whether you are or not.

Eye Contact

Eye contact is associated with honesty, trustworthiness, sincerity, confidence—all the traits you strive for on your way to becoming a great business communicator. We like people who look us in the eye. Whether speaking to large groups or one-on-one, eye contact is critical. This is the main reason preparation (Simple Secret #3) is so important, so we can avoid breaking that contact to read from notes or slides. But how long should you maintain eye contact? A general rule of thumb is to maintain eye contact long enough to register the color of your listener's eyes.

Hand Gestures

I'm Italian. That means I use my hands—a lot. Great business communicators use their hands too. Hand gestures, used sparingly and appropriately, can energize a presentation.

Dr. David McNeill at the University of Chicago is known for his exhaustive research in the area of hand gestures. His research has shown that gestures and language are intimately connected. Dr. McNeill told me that the use of gestures can help presenters speak better by clearing up their thought process. Yes, he says, it actually takes concentrated effort *not* to use gestures. Keeping your hands still "takes away from the rest of your mental capacities."

Dr. McNeill has found that very disciplined, rigorous, and confident thinkers use hand gestures that reflect the clarity of their thinking, a "window to their thought process." Understanding the power of hand gestures can help you stand apart.

Here are three simple pieces of advice, based on my conversations with Dr. McNeill.

1 Use gestures

Don't be afraid to use your hands in the first place. "Actors never leave gestures to chance," says McNeill. All great business speakers use hand gestures that are appropriate to the content of their message. Don't be afraid to use them. The simplest fix for a "stiff" presentation is simply to pull your hands out of your pockets—and to use them!

2 Use gestures sparingly

Okay, now that I've told you to use hand gestures, I'm going to suggest you don't use them that much! McNeill urges caution. Don't go overboard. Too many gestures at each and every point in your presentation will make it seem as though you're stepping in as traffic cop at a big-city intersection. That leads to the final piece of advice.

3 Use gestures at key moments

McNeill has found that great speakers are more inclined to use definitive and purposeful gestures during "key moments in the discourse." In other words, if it's important, use your hands to reinforce the point. I recall working with a senior executive who ran a division for one of the world's most famous brands. He was preparing a presentation for an internal competition where executives were invited to pitch ideas. Everyone knew it was a stepping-stone to the C-suite. I encouraged him to practice over and over for days. Specifically, I wanted his gestures to be grander and bigger since he would be on a large stage in front of hundreds of people. He came in second place, which, in a company of one hundred thousand employees, raised his status considerably. The presentation got him noticed. He's now next in line to be the CEO of one of the world's largest consumer brands.

SIMPLE SECRET #9

WEAR IT WELL

> **"You should always dress to suit who you are trying to work with."**
>
> —MARK CUBAN

James Citrin runs the global technology and communications practice for the world's largest private executive search firm, Spencer Stuart. The firm is responsible for 60 percent of Fortune 500 CEO placements. Citrin knows what to look for in an executive. More importantly, he knows what modern boards of directors are looking for in today's corporate leaders.

"You cannot lead without good communications," said Citrin.

"How much emphasis do you place on packaging, especially how one looks?" I asked Citrin.

"Nobody would talk about it as important, but it's important," Citrin said. "Does the candidate project neatness? Physically, are they what you expect? Do they dress appropriately to fit the culture? Are they well-groomed? People respond to all these things. There is a bound of acceptable physical presentation. That's not to say that all good decisions happen within bounds, but in terms of getting the nod, the odds are against you if you are outside the bounds."

"If someone you interview for a top position has a commanding presence and dresses well, what does that tell you?" I asked.

"If someone like that walks into the room, it causes you to relax and mentally check that box," Citrin said.

"They look the part. They've passed the first hurdle. Now let's move on." Pass the first hurdle. It's critical to winning 'em over.

"I decided early on that I would wear bright colors because being a woman in a man's world, I wanted to stand apart from the pack," Barbara Corcoran once told me. "I blended in too nicely with the navy blue or gray suits, so I started wearing red suits. In a room of five hundred people, they could pick me out. I've since gotten away from red. Now I dress in coral, orange, strong pinks—very bright colors. It draws the eye and holds people's attention."

The Perfect Package

As someone who runs the largest job fair for women, Tory Johnson knows what potential employers are looking for in a new hire. Johnson says packaging counts. If a recruiter is evaluating two equal candidates, it would only be human nature for the recruiter to consider the candidate who looks more put together.

According to Johnson, "Not only does that candidate have the right skills and experience, but the one who is put together better will be a better representative for your company. It would be naive to assume that it doesn't count." Johnson has some wardrobe advice for readers of this book, especially women, who want to pitch, promote, or present themselves in business situations or job interviews:

1 If in doubt about what to wear, stick to the conservative side. "You can never go wrong with basics. It doesn't mean you have to wear a skirt suit. Pants are perfectly acceptable in just about every line of work today. But it would be a pair of business pants or nice slacks over jeans to just about any type of professional event. Avoid clothes that are so obviously tight that someone would make a comment about it or even have a comment in their own mind."

2 Don't go heavy on the makeup or perfume. "A simpler, more natural appearance carries you far. Sometimes less is more. I don't mean that women should avoid makeup or perfume. But avoid excess."

3 Pay attention to details. They count. "No scuffed shoes or missing buttons. Little things like that. Earrings that are too big and flashy for a professional setting. So many times, I will see someone who looks impeccably dressed and they have scuffed shoes and it ruins the look. I hope your professionalism isn't judged on the condition or style of your shoes, but we do live in a society that is obsessed with looks and physical features. So if you have the ability to take two minutes to shine your shoes, it makes sense to go the extra mile."

4 Finally, dress appropriately. "It's important to understand your audience at any given time. If you're going to a casual networking event, you're not going to show up there with high heels and a cocktail dress. You'll want to be appropriate to that setting."

a. *Great communicators dress a little better than everybody else.*

b. *Great communicators dress well and dress appropriately for the occasion or industry.*

c. *Great communicators dress to complement their features, skin tone, and personal brand.*

A CEO Trainer for CEOs

Speakers who work out regularly look the part. They have more energy, better posture, and exude more confidence than most others who don't exercise. Scott Norton, the founder and CEO of AXIS Personal Trainers in Menlo Park, California, isn't surprised. Norton blew out his knee during his first year of playing football for the University of Utah. Turning a setback into an opportunity, Norton spent the next three years as a strength coach. After graduating, Norton spent another five years as a personal trainer before opening up his own center that caters to top executives in the San Francisco Bay area. In true Silicon Valley fashion, a venture capitalist even provided Norton the capital to open his facility. He has had more than one thousand clients who work with fifty-five trainers—the best trainers Norton could recruit from around the world.

I spoke to Norton as we stood on the training floor of the Menlo Park facility, surrounded by a flurry of sweat and activity and bodies in motion—the clanging of weights behind us, the whirring of treadmills to our left, a trainer pushing his client to perform "two more reps" to our right. Some of his clients, among the wealthiest and most powerful executives in the San Francisco Bay area, hit the gym by 6:00 a.m. for workouts that last one to one and a half hours.

"Why do these busy professionals carve out so much time to work out?" I asked Norton.

"Carmine, they have no choice. Fitness is part of the plan for the way they're going to live their life. They have to prepare their bodies to handle the demands of everyday life. They get up at six and work until midnight sometimes. They fly around the world, five or six countries in a week. They travel and they work. They can't afford not to workout. If they don't train, they will not have the strength, endurance, and ability to think on their feet."

Norton continues, "They're communicating and presenting all day—talking to clients, customers, employees, vendors—it's never ending. Their bodies have to be able to handle it. They need strength, control, and flexibility."

"When it comes to speaking and presenting, can you see a big difference between those CEOs committed to fitness and those who are not?" I asked Norton.

"Absolutely. I see enthusiasm, passion, eye contact, posture, and confidence. With these individuals, life doesn't get easier. It's important they prepare their bodies to handle it. Over the years, the body breaks down. After the age of twenty-five, your body will lose about five pounds of muscle every ten years. But if you do strength training, you don't lose it, you increase it—the bones, ligaments, and muscles all benefit. You'll have better posture. Better posture makes you look and feel more confident—you'll smile more and radiate leadership. Executives train to perform at their highest level. Without it, you'll look and sound like a dud during interviews, presentations, or board of director meetings. The executive who trains regularly will look and feel energized. He's passionate. He radiates energy. He makes his listeners feel alive!"

Great communicators look like the great speakers that they are. They dress well, they're well-groomed, and they're in great shape. Do the same. Remember, you're competing against them.

Now that we've covered the basics of packaging the spokesperson, it's time to reveal the tenth Simple Secret.

PART

4

LEAVE 'EM
WANTING MORE

Now that you've learned how to talk, walk, and look
like a leader, it's time to reveal the last Simple Secret
that will make your transformation complete. In this
last part, you'll hear from business professionals who
are compelling to listen to because they continue to
be relevant to twenty-first-century audiences. People
want to hear from them because they know they'll
learn something new. Everyone wants to leave your
talk having learned something they didn't know before.

In this section, you'll learn:

- how to captivate your audience every time and leave them wanting more by keeping your message current,

- how great corporate speakers continue to transform themselves with every presentation and excel at communicating change,

- how to keep the power in your PowerPoint presentations, and

- the single greatest secret to take away from this book.

It's time to reveal the Simple Secret that will make your transformation complete. Are you ready? Let's go!

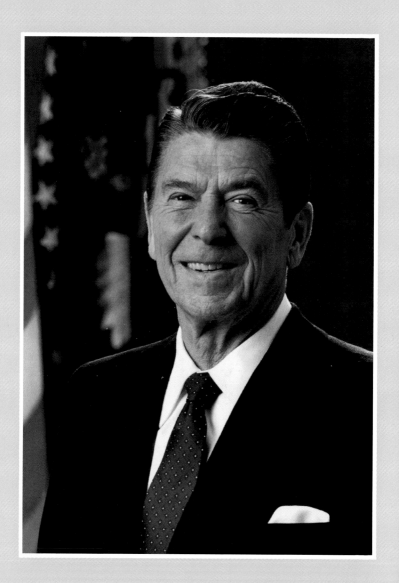

SIMPLE SECRET #10

REINVENT YOURSELF

> **"You can't act like a know-it-all;**
> **you have to be a learn-it-all."**
> —SATYA NADELLA

Ronald Reagan, "the Great Communicator," wasn't always a great communicator. He built his public-speaking skills over time. In fact, it was only after Reagan's acting career began to draw to a close that he developed the speaking skills that made him famous.

In the 1950s, General Electric hired Reagan to host a weekly television show and to give speeches around the country on behalf of the company. It was during that time that Reagan polished his delivery. Reagan once said that in his eight years at GE, he had visited 139 plants and spent four thousand hours talking to thousands of employees. Great speaking takes relentless optimism, energy, and practice.

"I'll Be Back…As a Master Presenter"

Another actor turned political leader is Arnold Schwarzenegger. He spoke little English when he first arrived in America. A studio actually hired an actor to provide the voice-over for Schwarzenegger's voice in the movie *Hercules in New York*. Schwarzenegger attacked his language barrier with the same razor-like focus and determination he brings to everything else in his life. I covered Schwarzenegger's campaign for California governor while working as a correspondent for CBS. I learned that Schwarzenegger was *not* a natural presenter. He had to work at it. Schwarzenegger approached the task as a great athlete. Just as Michael Jordan practiced harder than most of his peers to dominate basketball and just as Jerry Rice was the hardest-working man in football, Schwarzenegger approached public speaking as his next goal to conquer.

Schwarzenegger's closest friends told me that he gave more and more speeches in the mid- to late 1990s because he was preparing to raise his visibility as a political leader. That means he sought out every speaking opportunity he could find. Schwarzenegger knew, in one way or another, that the next phase of his life would require that he be more visible and more comfortable as a communicator in front of a live audience—not a movie camera. He didn't quite know what he would do next—more charity work, direct movies, or run for office. But he knew whatever he did would require more public speaking. Giving as many speeches as he could was a fun way to improve.

Do you seek out every opportunity to practice your presentations?

Communication starts at the top. If salespeople or employees fail to do a good job communicating to customers, it's a sure sign those at the top fail to communicate to their subordinates. If you're at the top, or if you want to get there, make sure great communication starts with you.

None of the secrets revealed in this book will do anything to improve your skill as a communicator in your personal or professional life unless you believe you belong in the same category as the men and women interviewed and profiled in this book.

What do you say to yourself when you're presenting? Do you tell yourself that you have an exciting message that will change the lives of the people in your audience, or do you knock yourself down by saying nobody's interested in your subject and in you as a speaker? If you hope to win over your audience, you've got to think like great communicators.

Until this point, your story has been my passion. It's now time for you to reveal the magnificent message behind your own service, product, company, or cause. It's time for your story to become your passion. It's time to take your rightful place alongside the world's greatest business communicators, winning over your customers, colleagues, peers, and prospects. You belong. Believe you belong. Remember, when you change the way you see yourself as a speaker, the speaker your audience sees will change.

"As long as there is communication, everything can be solved."

—ROBERT TRUJILLO

ACKNOWLEDGMENTS

I set out to write a book that reveals the simple secrets of great business communicators who inspire everyone in their personal and professional lives. I'm grateful to all those who gave generously of their time to shape this work. You've proven to me, your employees, your customers, and your investors why you hold a rightful place among the world's top business leaders. More than two dozen CEOs, executives, entrepreneurs, and experts offered their time and wisdom, and I thank each and every one of them.

I'm also grateful to the team behind Simple Truths at Sourcebooks. Acquisitions editor Meg Gibbons inspired me to write a small book with a big impact.

One could not be blessed with a more supportive family. My parents, Francesco and Giuseppina, never placed limits on my dreams; Tino, Donna, Fran, and Nick, thanks for all you did and all you continue to do. My in-laws, Ken and Patty Cook, deserve the credit for raising the greatest woman I know. Vanessa, you're my angel and my true inspiration.

ABOUT THE AUTHOR

CARMINE GALLO is a popular keynote speaker and international bestselling author whose books have been translated into more than forty languages. Carmine teaches a course in leadership and communication in the office of executive education at Harvard University. His ideas have influenced CEOs, executives, and entrepreneurs at the world's most admired brands. Carmine lives in wine country in Northern California with his wife and two daughters.

NEW! Only from Simple Truths®

IGNITE READS

spark impact in just one hour

IGNITE READS IS A NEW SERIES OF 1-HOUR READS WRITTEN BY WORLD-RENOWNED EXPERTS!

These captivating books will help you become the best version of yourself, allowing for new opportunities in your personal and professional life. Accelerate your career and expand your knowledge with these powerful books written on today's hottest ideas.

TRENDING BUSINESS AND PERSONAL GROWTH TOPICS

 Read in an hour or less

 Leading experts and authors

 Bold design and captivating content